Limitless Loving Leadership

Jessica R. Dreistadt

Limitless Loving Leadership
© 2013, 2016 Jessica R. Dreistadt.

All rights reserved. No part of this publication may be reproduced, distributed, or transmitted in any form or by any means, including photocopying, recording, or other electronic or mechanical methods, without the prior written permission of the publisher, except in the case of brief quotations embodied in critical reviews and certain other noncommercial uses permitted by copyright law. Requests for permission to use or reproduce material from this book should be directed to utopia@fruitioncoalition.com.

ISBN 978-1537727592

The Fruition Coalition
Lehigh Valley, PA
www.fruitioncoalition.com
www.jessicardreistadt.com

Table of Contents

Forward	4
Introduction	6
Ego	11
Humility	15
Authenticity	18
Detachment	22
Deconstruction	26
Choice	30
Understanding	33
Weakness	37
Vulnerability	41
Value	45
Beauty	48
Expectations	52
Commitment	55
Failure	57
Temperance	61
Listening	66
Fortitude	69
Patience	72
Defeat	75
Transparency	78
Optimism	81
Flow	84
Flexibility	87
Fear	90
Self Care	94
Intuition	98
Openness	101
Wisdom	105
Planning and Reflection Worksheets	109

Forward

I started writing Limitless Loving Leadership in 2009 when I was going through a very difficult time at work. Thinking through and writing about positive, loving leadership was therapeutic for me. It provided me with a constructive outlet for my hopes and dreams that seemed to be trampled upon by my situation at the time. It helped me to explore and make decisions about the kind of leader I was, wanted to be, and could be.

The book originally included 100 chapters. I whittled those down to 50 and only completed 28 of them. Those original, unedited essays were published on my blog, The Activist's Muse, starting in the summer of 2012. The topics were not by any means strategically selected; they merely reflect what I felt most comfortable writing about at the time. Those posts, and this book, are therefore not meant to be taken as an exhaustive volume, but rather the beginning of a conversation.

It has been more than seven years since I first started writing Limitless Loving Leadership. Over that time, I have learned a lot. I have had even more difficult and devastating experiences as a leader. I have pushed myself harder than ever. I have completed more than half of a doctorate. When I read through the original text, I think things like, "oh my goodness, did I really think that?" and 'I sure have learned a lot since then!' Overall, I find that the Limitless Loving Leadership essays were highly prescriptive. I now think, and know in my heart, that prescriptive leadership sucks. Good leaders create openings for emergence, they create waves, they provoke exploration; they don't dictate. The authoritarian tone of those original 28 essays now makes me feel uncomfortable. At times, I also found those essays to be too linear and simplistic. Yet, there are some really good ideas and beautiful prose in the book that I believe merit our attention. This is why I chose to publish Limitless Loving Leadership, despite its serious limitations as a text, in 2013.

My first inclination was to make significant edits to what I had written to reflect my current thinking. But in an effort to be an authentic leader, much in the spirit of Limitless Loving Leadership, I reprinted the original text along with my 2013 reflections. This demonstrated what I observed and learned about myself and the world over those four years. I intended for it to show that I, as a leader, was vulnerable and open to learning. When that book was published, I projected that I might update this text in another four years with yet deeper and more profound insights into the complexities of leadership. It is now three years later and I am doing just that.

This book represents an integration of those original 2009 essays, my candid reflections in 2013, and where I am today. Each essay has been reshaped to reflect a more comprehensive and complex understanding of leadership, one that can only be discovered through time and a great deal of tribulation. In doing so, I hope that the book is less prescriptive and less linear, instead mobilizing and liberating our diverse visions of the leader within.

After each essay, I offer questions and space for you to reflect upon your own leadership philosophy and practice. The end of the book has daily, weekly, monthly, and annual planning and reflection sheets to guide the integration of limitless loving leadership — whatever that means to you — into your everyday life.

Introduction

Limitations exist for many reasons: to protect us from physical or emotional danger; to conserve and allocate limited resources; and to balance the otherwise insatiable needs and desires of human beings in relationship. They serve functions that are both natural and imposed; they can be real or illusory. Limitations can feel like barriers, constraints, or obstacles that interfere with our desire for, and ability to pursue, human liberation.

While the limitations in our lives may seem endless, the love in our hearts need not be. Limitless loving leadership offers an antidote to the feelings of powerlessness, cynicism, despair, and frustration that can block even the most creative and cheerful of leaders from time to time.

Leadership is the process of resisting and redefining limitations; yet, we live in a world where limitations seem to be limitless. Love can help us transcend those spiritual, emotional, physical, and intellectual barriers that inhibit our true nature by developing and activating deeper self-awareness, community harmonization, and divine connection. We need to recognize and question the many ways that limitations are internally and socially constructed to accommodate our fears and disappointments.

The ideas in this book apply to leaders of all kinds — mothers who are in charge of unruly (or well-behaved) children, CEOs of transnational corporations, grassroots community group leaders, teachers, coaches, neighbors, and friends. We all have the opportunity to exercise leadership when we make decisions that impact other human beings and our planet. This typically happens hundreds of times every day. *Limitless Loving Leadership will* help you cultivate awareness about the many ways all human beings assume the role of leader, regardless of the magnitude of each person's impact, and to be more intentional about the decisions you make on a daily basis.

Limitless Loving Leadership is based on five infinite, renewable resources that actually multiply whenever they are used and shared with others:

- **Love** — the light that shines from within our souls and radiates through our every thought and action

- **Compassion** — the understanding that all living things are interconnected and that we share a yearning for lovingkindness

- **Wisdom** — the collective experience and knowledge of ourselves, our communities, and the universe

- **Sincerity** — the ability to be honest, authentic, and straightforward with ourselves and others especially during those times when it feels uncomfortable

- **Hope** — a sense that the future will be glorious and recognition that we, as leaders, have an instrumental role to play in realizing this dream

Our approach to limitless loving leadership will be based on three philosophical ideas. It is:

- **Interdisciplinary** — leadership practice is strengthened through the exploration, inclusion, and integration of diverse epistemologies, ideologies, and methodologies

- **Holistic** — all things are connected, often in interesting and unexpected ways

- **Fluid** — matter, thoughts, and interactions are in a constant state of motion which reminds us to be evolutionary, flexible, and detached from what we believe the truth to be at any given moment

Scientific inquiry in the academy calls for rigid definitions and operationalization of concepts. As a doctoral student and future keeper of the discipline, I fully value and accept the responsibility of that approach. *Limitless Loving Leadership* is a different kind of experiment — one that engages not only our minds, but also our hearts and our souls. Our definition of limitless loving leadership allows room for mystery, wonder, and imagination.

I have come to the painful (not yet transcendent) realization that I am nothing and I know nothing. I do not profess that this book will make you more rich or successfully or happy. As Gil Scott-Heron said in The Revolution will not be Televised, "the revolution will not make you look five pounds thinner." Neither will this book. What will *Limitless Loving Leadership* help you become or achieve? That's up to you. My hope is that *Limitless Loving Leadership* will serve as a source of inspiration, encouragement, and amusement for any and all people who embrace and live the joyous struggle of leading and facilitating change. By the time you are finished reading this book, I hope you are able to not only step outside of "the box" but to realize that the box was never really there in the first place — it was only a figment of our collective imaginations.

Limitless Loving Leadership is based on the assumption that our personal and professional lives are deeply intertwined and that changing who we are as a person has a profound impact on our professional life. This, in turn, impacts the communities and society in which we live. At times when writing this book, I felt overwhelmed with sadness. I realized that I am not living up to my potential in some areas and that I often feel uncertain about my next steps. If you feel resistance as you work through this book, spend some time with your feelings and consider discussing what you have learned with a friend (or professional, if needed). I have not yet developed the maturity to fully employ all of the concepts in this book all of the time; it is a reflection of my aspirational self. My goal is to fully align my values and intentions with action. We are on this journey together.

I spent a few days with His Holiness the Dalai Lama as he lectured to a large crowd at Lehigh University in the summer of 2008. He extolled the many virtues of Buddhism and its practical application to diverse daily matters. He acknowledged that not all tenets of this particular belief system would be welcome by all. He told the audience that if there were aspects of his teachings not to their liking then, and I quote, "Fuck it. No problem."

Like the Dalai Lama, I encourage you to sort through the material in this book, use what is relevant, meaningful, or useful to you, and leave the rest behind. No problem.

Your Response—Introduction

What does limitless loving leadership mean to you?

How are you a limitless loving leader?

What infinite resources are available to you as a leader? How can you share them with others?

How have your personal and professional experiences shaped your understanding of leadership?

Ego

Ego imbalances can be rampant in leadership circles. You know who you are: the board member with a personal agenda; the coach on a power trip; the supervisor who speaks with two mouths and listens with one ear. Although you may not fit into one of these archetypes, there are times when all of us suffer from ego saturation. This is when our ego leads us to act in a way that is contrary to our highest values under the guise of self-protection and self-preservation. When our ego overwhelms other aspects of who we are, there is an imbalance.

When others try to hurt us, we sometimes pull out our ego shield to fend them off or hide. When they really hurt us, we may grasp our ego sword to poke at them or slice them down. As a leader, we must always think and act offensively, strategically, and holistically rather than reacting to the situation. Keep that shield and sword for emergencies only.

The ego can serve as a barrier to insulate, separate, and isolate us from the radiant energy of the universe and from that of other people. This can be a protective or destructive device depending on the circumstance. When our health or well-being is threatened, an ego-driven response keeps us safe. When our sense of self-righteousness is challenged, our ego severs relationships and natural life processes with the unintended outcome of further isolation and feelings of abandonment on both sides.

I tend to be a quiet, humble person. I am quite aware of this, and am equally aware of how other leaders may misinterpret my peaceful countenance. When I enter a meeting with other leaders with whom I only have an ancillary relationship, I know that some of them may be under the impression that I am weak, inexperienced, or unintelligent. I therefore tend to feel defensive when another leader says something to imply that my ideas are less valid or important than theirs. An ego-driven response in this situation might get my point across, but it would also make me look and feel selfish and insecure. Calmly explaining a thorough justification for my idea would instead reflect my true nature: that of a confident, compassionate, and collaborative community leader.

The ego masques our true feelings, values, beliefs, motivations, and ambitions. In the mental space where we navigate and negotiate the characteristics that distinguish us from others, who we truly are or ought to be can become confused when our ego is directing and controlling our thoughts. The ego defines us by making comparisons to, and judgments about, people we admire and despise; our soul understands and celebrates our individuality based on our personal experiences, character, thoughts, and actions. By transcending the ego and tapping into our souls, there are no externally defined limits on who we can be or what we can accomplish.

The space we subconsciously use to accommodate our ego is where we accumulate hurt, disappointment, and feelings of inadequacy. This clutter challenges our ability to lead with love and compassion by triggering ego-driven responses. Yet sometimes we choose to dwell in this dreary, horrible place. Perhaps it feels comfortable; familiar thought patterns, even those that are counterproductive or hurtful, are in the realm of what we know and have a sense of being able to control. The more time we spend in our ego space, the longer we yearn to be there to negate the negativity we have stockpiled — and off we go into the black hole of the downward spiral. Why not just bust out of your ego box and draw in the good directly?

By releasing our ego, we open up unlimited possibilities and more opportunities to find joy and unexpected surprises in ourselves, the people with whom we work, and the process of experiencing our vocation. When you become aware of your ego interfering in your interactions with others and interrupting your intuitive soulful response, imagine releasing it like a bird that will fly to a nearby tree branch where it can watch over you. Liberate your mind as your ego seeps out of your body and into the air; watch it transform into positive energy all around you. Imagine yourself walking about surrounded with sparkles and sweetly chirping birds; you are safe, whole, and vibrant. Remember that you can always pull out your ego sword and shield — just in case.

Your Response—Ego

How does your ego impact your leadership?

How do you know when you are experiencing ego saturation?

How do you respond when others are experiencing ego saturation?

What does it mean to be selfish? Selfless? How are these related?

Humility

My mom always says that regardless of a person's life experience or cultural background, we can all recognize the smell of feet. I add that we all have stinky feet — and sometimes other body parts, too! Leaders are certainly not above this human phenomenon. I know that my feet stink — and that yours probably do, too...especially on a sweltering summer day.

All human beings, even leaders, are rife with multiple faults and shortcomings. Take me, for example. I am a workaholic multi-tasker, and I make mistakes all of the time. Although I have been entrusted with great responsibilities in my leadership, and rightfully so, I am not immune to foibles resulting from poor judgment, miscommunication, or lack of information on occasion.

Think of the many ways your humanity is revealed to you on a daily basis. When you wake up, you are confronted with morning breath and ripe armpits. You trip on a crack in the concrete and fall flat on your face. You forget to put twenty-five cents in the parking meter and get a ticket for fifty dollars. You spill hot coffee all over your new outfit, and that of the co-worker that you just bumped into, in your hurry to get to a very important meeting on time. You mistake Mr. Married with Five Children for Mr. Wonderful. Oops and oops again.

We are all perfectly imperfect. Me, you, our co-workers, our colleagues, our families, and people in our community. We all stink, we all make mistakes, and we are all suffering and struggling in our own way.

When your humanity is unintentionally revealed to you or exposed to others, show yourself some compassion. Let light and love fill your heart. Find humor in the situation if possible and if not, look for a lesson to discover the situation's meaning. When others around you reveal their humanity, extend the same courtesy to them.

Feelings of embarrassment, guilt, and remorse, which tend to surface, resurface, and resurface again, are of not necessarily useful when experienced by anyone involved with your organization. These serve as a reminder, perhaps, of our humanity; however, without analysis and positive transformation, these negative feelings can be overwhelming and counterproductive. Walking the rocky road of life with great humility expedites understanding, forgiveness, and healing.

Your Response—Humility

What does humility mean to you as a leader?

How do you reveal your humanity to others as a leader?

How do you respond when others reveal their humanity to you?

How do negative emotions influence your leadership — for better or worse?

Authenticity

I often feel the need to separate my personal and professional identities. They are not necessarily inconsistent; however, I fear that my quirkiness and eccentricities might bemuse, offend, or alienate some people with whom it is important for me to maintain a professional relationship.

I have several close personal friends who I initially met and got to know on a professional basis. When these relationships start to cross that line, I always feel a bit of anxiety as I start to slowly reveal the 'real me.' The risk of destroying a professional relationship because a trial friendship has gone awry is one that merits careful consideration.

As I mature and have additional experiences exploring a variety of interpersonal relationships, I increasingly understand the value of being sincere and genuine right from the beginning and at all times. Does anyone really care that I am a socialist cat lady who occasionally enjoys listening to thrash metal?

In fact, these distinguishing characteristics may make me more intriguing and appealing to those trapped in the mundanity of 9 to 5. My uniqueness and individuality set me apart from the crowd and provide cues for others to remember who I am. And for those who find me offensive, that's just too bad.

Hiding my true nature would be wasteful. Eventually, most people will find out something personal about me through the grapevine (if not the Internet). If a colleague finds this information to be unsavory, we can cut to the chase and terminate the relationship before it gets too complicated — if that is the other person's true desire. Sharing all aspects of my personality, beliefs, and activities may help another person learn something or develop a new interest. Withholding personal information limits opportunities for people to get to know wonderful me — and for me to get to know wonderful them in exchange.

When we piece together the many aspects of our lives, it is like melting chunks of cheese in a pot. It all combines to make one sauce that is our unique essence. Our spirit is the heat that melts the cheese which we use to flavor life by pouring it over everything we taste. Before pouring our sauce over someone else's bread, we ought to let them know what they are about to eat.

Appearances can be deceiving. Bleu cheese, which looks moldy and smells like something unsavory, is widely considered to be a lovely delicacy with many culinary uses. I may appear to be a stuffy, serious organizational leader from afar, but inside I am a dynamic woman with extraordinary passions, hopes, and dreams. My fear may manifest as confidence; my insecurities as competencies. Taking the time to experience and develop a deeper understanding of others usually reveals many wonderful surprises.

I also have a few skeletons in my closet that most people do not know about. They all represent a learning experience that strengthened my character, expanded my capabilities, and fueled my growth. There is a direct and concrete application between difficult personal experiences and my ability to effectively lead. Yet, our society does not encourage sharing these stories. There is a stigma associated with 'abnormal' experiences – yet anyone who has truly lived has had a preponderance of them. By exploring and sharing these experiences with others in a safe environment, perhaps with others who have had a similar experience, we can expand our understanding and develop deeper connections with others.

Our experiences, which include those that we may not be so proud of, make us who we are. They shape our goals, motivations, and values. Being honest with ourselves and others about where we are coming from and where we hope to go channels our collective energy into strategies and activities that directly support our deepest desires and dreams.

We can also let go of the various iterations of identity that have attached themselves to our egos throughout the years and instead discover a more fluid sense of self, deeply rooted in our values and purpose. We can integrate all of those identities by connecting the common threads and weaving the divergences together into something even greater.

Your Response—Authenticity

What is authentic leadership?

How do you integrate your true self into your work?

How do you create space spaces for others to be authentic with you?

How do you allow your true self to flow and continually emerge?

Detachment

Everyone's brain is tricked into having biased thoughts at one time or another. We organize information into categories based on what we see, are told, and directly experience. When we do not have exhaustive information and generalize personal experiences, our beliefs may not accurately reflect the totality of potentiality and reality.

Having worked in social service organizations and education for nearly two decades, I am continually shocked when I discover other leaders' beliefs about the people who are actively engaged in these systems. Leaders, who make crucial decisions about how resources will be used to meet community needs, often have biased and even prejudiced beliefs about people who live in poverty and people of color.

I once attended a day-long character education workshop for educators where one of the presenters, who represented a leadership education organization, talked about values-based leadership. He also repeatedly stated that it is important to teach this to children from impoverished communities because when they go home they are in an environment where there are no values. Unfortunately, this is a myth that I have often seen taught to educators and social service providers. I couldn't help but wonder if this gentleman had ever been in one of those communities, or how many parents and children he really took the time to get to know. If you are working to alleviate poverty or to provide a service to people who are impoverished, do you think living in the condition of poverty is the result of a deficit of character? Carefully examine your attitudes and beliefs toward others — co-workers, subordinates, volunteers, interns, customers, program participants, vendors, and colleagues — to uncover and understand your bias.

Forget about what you think you know so that you can emerge fearless into the realm of what is possible. See things for what they are, not for what you think they are or want them to be. Approach every moment, person, and circumstance with a new mind. Base your understanding of each individual person that you meet on what that person reveals to you rather than your accumulated knowledge of people you find to be similar in one way or another. Live in the present moment rather than the past and be open to all of the possibilities that life has to offer.

If, through a process of deep reflection and examination, you discover that you do hold a biased or prejudiced belief, forgive yourself to overcome shame and grief. Recognize that it is healthy to change your beliefs in response to receiving new information or understanding; this is personal growth.

When we are driving a car to a specific destination, we usually have several choices about how to get there. Sometimes we choose a shortcut because it will get us to our destination faster. As our brain develops, taking too many shortcuts out of convenience shortchanges our learning processes and maturation. As you have new interpersonal and life experiences, allow your brain to form new neurological routes. Take the scenic route once in a while and gather new ideas and insights to inform your decisions for those times when it is necessary to take a shortcut.

By living in the present and continually developing the basis of our understanding on complex information, the possibilities for growth and change emerge. When we truly understand the intricacies of humanity, our ability to envision possibilities and work toward an idealized future is enhanced.

Your Response—Detachment

What beliefs or feelings limit your leadership?

Where do those beliefs and feelings come from?

How can you integrate those beliefs and feelings into a greater whole?

How do you remain open when coming into contact with new ideas or information?

Deconstruction

Our families and communities of origin provide much of the framework through which we understand our world. We learn a lot about leadership, and sometimes about how not to lead, through our families. Ideas about life's purpose and meaning evolve over generations and we receive bits and pieces of this wisdom formally through instruction as well as informally through observation and interactions. This collection of ideas changes over time as wisdom is inadvertently lost and as new ideas from the outside world are introduced to supplant previous worldviews.

Although we sometimes take this information for granted, as it seems to have always been a part of us, we have great love and respect for our families, neighbors, teachers, and others who shared our formative years. For some of us, it can be difficult to even think about questioning the basic premises beneath the surface of our family's and community's beliefs. For others, new ideas about the world and life are both welcome and exciting. And sometimes, we subconsciously continue family and community beliefs, behaviors, and ideas without thought to whether or not these things are actually relevant to our own personal lives.

Our families and communities shape our values and beliefs and the wisdom of previous generations provide a great amount of information from which we can draw as we make decisions. We can build upon what our families teach us and transfer this knowledge to the next generation.

An important part of growing up, which ought to be done before assuming a leadership position, is determining who we truly are and developing the ability to take or leave what has been presented to us by our families and home communities. Our families, friends, and communities can hold us back with love and a desire to keep us within their comfort zone. Intentionally changing family patterns can be difficult, even devastating. Others who belong to our group may feel as though we have left them behind when we choose to live our lives differently than they have.

It is possible to remain connected to these important people while having our own lives and identity. The stronger your personal identity, the easier it will be for you to hold your own while demonstrating genuine compassion and love for others. This will allow you to make decisions unencumbered by the complications of the past.

My grandfather has a cousin who went to prestigious Lehigh University. My grandfather and other cousins often stated that he thought he was, "hot shit" because of it. I, too, went to Lehigh University for my second master's degree and I will be the first person in my family to complete a doctorate. Does this make me hot shit too? Not really. I think it makes me ambitious, visionary, and hardworking, just like the rest of my family. Achieving my educational goals should give my family something to celebrate and build upon rather than divide us and cause antagonism.

Although I am not yet a parent, I often think about the experiences that I would like for my children to have. I want them to experience all of the magnificent things I did with my family as a child, but few of the non-constructive challenges. I also want to share the personal interests and experiences that I acquired outside of our family with them. I anticipate that they will share my natural curiosity and will have many formative experiences outside of our family, which they can share with the rest of us through storytelling and perhaps a few adventures.

Our families teach us many meaningful lessons about humanity, society, and ourselves. They also unintentionally pass along their limiting beliefs. We can bring great honor to our families by taking what they have taught us and sharing it with the rest of the world but also by bringing back to our families the many things we learn as we navigate the outside world.

According to epigenetic research, our genetic code can actually be transformed through our experiences. In other words, the more exposure we have to diverse ideas and experiences, the stronger our evolutionary potential as individuals, families, and human beings. Although a bona fide epigeneticist might not fully agree with my interpretation of this concept, I hope we can all agree that our family and community legacies are strengthened, and the more beautiful future that we all desire can be realized, by connecting and integrating a variety of perspectives and life experiences.

Your Response—Deconstruction

What has your family taught you about leadership?

What family traditions will you transform? How?

How have you transcended the limitations of your family and expanded/strengthened its evolutionary potential)? How do you include others in this personal evolution?

What stories related to leadership can be found within your family? How does this influence your ideas about leadership and your leadership practice?

Choice

Before we are even born, our families, close family friends, and neighbors all have their own ideas about who we ought to be. Our families will decide where we live, what kind of clothes we will wear, where we go to school, what kind of food we will eat, and what opportunities we may have in life with little effort on our part. Sometimes, they even have ideas about our personal characteristics and our careers. When they choose our careers (or what careers we will not have if they have anything to do with it), this is based an idea about what kind of meaning that career holds for them and these feelings can be transferred along with the message about the action to be taken to achieve this goal. They may truly love us and wish the best for us, but their well wishes may not always be in our best interest, or in that of our community.

People who are not in our family may also have expectations for us throughout our lives. Teachers, supervisors, and friends get to know us and, based on their own experiences and expectations, form opinions of what we should and should not do or be. Even strangers sometimes form opinions of us based on appearances and limited interactions.

As a child, I was never encouraged to work in the nonprofit sector. I was not steered toward becoming an executive director until I gained sufficient experience and demonstrated competence as a nonprofit employee. Yet, I cannot imagine traveling along a different career path at that time in my life. This was a goal that I formulated based on my vision of how my skills could make the most significant contribution. Today, I find that many adults do not know what the nonprofit sector is or what various positions within the sector do. How could this be presented as a possibility to me if others were unaware of it even being an option?

I have had a few experiences of exclusion based upon my religion, gender, appearance, and social class throughout my life. These experiences did not inform me or shape my opportunities; rather, they revealed the prejudice and ignorance of those who set up and maintained these social parameters. When I am told that I cannot do something because of an irrelevant personal characteristic, I feel empowered to prove that person wrong by redefining expectations while honoring my personal skills, talents, values, and dreams. Collectively, we have the ability to overcome barriers to full participation in any system – with time, patience, perseverance, and resolve. As Kurtis Blow says in one of my favorite songs, *Throughout Your Years*, "with a little hard work and dedication, we'll pull together and rock the nation."

I certainly acknowledge that there are many oppressive, exclusionary systems throughout the world and that these are perpetuated by prejudicial beliefs and feelings of entitlement. I also acknowledge that this is unacceptable. We must do what we can to create meaningful opportunities for engagement and provide access to social and capital resources within existing systems and, when necessary, create new organizations and other social structures to realize inclusivity.

We are responsible for the decisions we make throughout our lives. We have to live with the consequences of the direction we choose. Refuse to let others choose for you.

Your Response—Choice

What have you learned from experiences of exclusion? How has this impacted your leadership?

How have you exceeded others' expectations for your career and your life?

How do you share your work with others in your family? What is your purpose for doing this?

What life decisions have been made for you, and what decisions have you made unintentionally based on your perceptions of others' expectations? How do you feel about these decisions?

Understanding

A lot of what we think and do stems from our subconscious feelings and beliefs. These are influenced by our experiences and personality as well as our understanding of our social position – past, present, and future. Social hierarchies influence the opportunities that are available to us and others as well as our perception of those opportunities. We may also hold beliefs about the types of opportunities that ought to be available to ourselves or others based on social position.

Think about the social groups to which you belong. These groups may include gender, age, religion, nationality, ethnicity, occupation, or income. For each group, think about stereotypical beliefs that have been revealed to you through either personal experience or the media. I'm sure you can make a list of opportunities that have been opened and closed to you and others like you as a result of your group affiliations.

Carefully examine how you feel when thinking about that list of prejudicial and discriminatory beliefs and practices. Do you feel angry? Sad? Proud? Think about how these feelings have infiltrated and influenced your subconscious reasoning, morphing your self-concept and restricting your behaviors.

Who we are can be defined both internally and externally and we have the power to transform those perceptions through our intentions and actions. As free flowing and open as I like to think I am, I really do hold a lot of limiting beliefs. These beliefs have come from my family, my friends, my co-workers, and my own interpretations of my circumstances. I am becoming more and more aware of these beliefs and perhaps that is the first step toward letting them go. Awareness is the first step toward transformation.

Being unintentionally prejudiced is a part of human nature. As a middle-aged woman, I would feel silly walking around in a miniskirt. Even though I am a beautiful person and I am just as hot, both literally and figuratively, as your average 25-year-old, it would be considered distasteful, if not disgusting, by some people (i.e. sexist, ageist creeps) for me to reveal myself in this way. This benign example illustrates just one of the many, many collective social rules that preside over our thoughts and actions.

As a woman with fair skin, I can freely enter and walk around most stores. I once visited a store with my 16-year-old African American G-ddaughter to buy her a keepsake from our vacation. We were meticulously followed as we browsed through the store. We both entered the store with a different expectation of what the experience might be like based on our social group membership. Although we had visited hundreds of stores without incident, I am certain that every time there was had been an underlying fear and anticipation of what might happen on her part without a second thought on mine.

Without even realizing it, we both continually manifested internalized oppression and privilege related to shopping over the years. It did not have a significant impact on our lives. In many other instances, internalized oppression and privilege can interfere with our ability to successfully interact with others and fully participate in social activities. Shopping may be a benign example of prejudice and discrimination, when there are institutional and political factors that have a much greater impact, but perhaps it is indicative of the everyday taken for granted things that limit us from the inside or out.

We have the ability to choose to accept or reject these limiting beliefs. We also have the ability to reposition our group both internally and externally to more appropriately reflect both reality and the group's collective hopes for the future.

As leaders, we should work both to transform and equalize social systems so that all have access to opportunities to do what is meaningful to them and to heal our personal relationships with the social structures that have effortlessly included or systematically excluded us. Transcending barriers such as these leads to more inclusive, healthy organizations and communities.

Your Response—Understanding

What limiting beliefs do you hold about yourself, others, and the world?

How do these beliefs influence your leadership?

What would your leadership be like without these limiting beliefs?

How can or will you set these limiting beliefs free?

Weakness

I am a controlling perfectionist who worries about everything that I can't control (which is just about everything) and obsesses about everything else. I always try to take on too much and refuse to accept help from others. These characteristics cause me a great deal of stress; I direct a lot of energy toward managing and, of course, trying to control them. But I also have learned a lot about myself and become a stronger person as a result of recognizing and gaining a deeper understanding of these weaknesses. By admitting that I have weaknesses, naming them, and increasing my awareness of their effect on my life, I have opened myself up to change and growth.

Control has definitely been a huge thing with me throughout my life. I am learning to let go as I grow older and wiser. By letting go, I make room for growth. When I attempt to control, which is really just an illusion, I hold myself back. Control is an attempt to live in the present based on what has happened in the past or expectations for the future. Letting go is being vulnerable and open to possibility right at this very moment.

Control can be difficult for leaders because we usually also have management responsibilities, and control is one of the underlying assumptions of management practice. Perhaps it isn't realistic to think that leaders can just let go and be vulnerable all of the time; however, doing so whenever we can may lead to even more miraculous results that we might have imagined on our own.

My deepest and most flexible strengths are most easily revealed when I examine and engage with my vulnerabilities. Working through our weaknesses provides us with opportunities to strengthen our character, expand our abilities, and develop self-confidence. In order to effectively change our ways, we may seek information or support from our peers, mentors, or even from new individuals or organizations. This leads to new and renewed trusted relationships, an expanded network, and a system to monitor and reinforce changes that we choose for ourselves.

Our weaknesses can feel prohibitive, frustrating, and overwhelming. Choose the path of the breakthrough rather than that of the breakdown. When you become aware of a weakness wreaking havoc in your life, recognize and seek to change your thoughts and behaviors.

What are your weaknesses? Think about those aspects of your personality, skills, and knowledge base that are yearning for cultivation. Use your strengths and competencies to develop these areas, seeking help as needed. Set incremental goals to monitor and document your success.

All human beings have self-defined weaknesses. In addition to dealing with your own needs, you may sometimes feel equally distressed about the weaknesses of others. Extend patience and compassion to others who are on their journey toward self-realization. Focus on strengths, develop complementary work teams to minimize the impact on your organization's results, and provide opportunities for ongoing learning and growth.

Allowing our weaknesses to surface may feel uncomfortable, but through this process we will find hope for the future, appreciation for what we have, and determination to achieve positive personal or organizational change. The arduous process of living through our weaknesses is a transformational growing pain.

Living and leading with love is not so much about struggle, but rather about surrender. Struggle is a story I keep telling myself about my life and I think in doing so I have overshadowed the many good things from both my past and my present. By truly surrendering and being vulnerable, we can both expand and flow. When we struggle, we constrict and get stuck. Understanding our weaknesses for what they are, and not artificially transforming them into strengths, is a valuable practice. To be vulnerable is to be comfortable with weakness and uncertainty. And that is a great source of strength.

Your Response—Weakness

What do you try to control? Why? What is the result of attempting to control things, ideas, or people?

What do you need to let go?

How can or will you surrender as a leader?

What does it mean to be weak? How does this resonate with your perception of leadership?

Vulnerability

Imagine yourself running down the street naked. Not a pretty thought? Don't worry, I'm not about to suggest you do something as extreme as that. There are more advantageous, and appropriate, means of exposing your vulnerability to others. This may include asking for help, admitting a mistake, or accepting failure.

When I was younger, I felt it was important to demonstrate my competence in order to build others' confidence in my ability to do a good job. This shortsighted behavior resulted in all sorts of problems including important files being thrown away and oversights on reports. Pretending to know everything was not only dishonest, it prevented me from learning and developing truly supportive relationships with my supervisors. I probably also looked foolish because nobody, not even the most intelligent people in the world, really know everything. That is an unrealistic expectation and an invitation for isolation and eventual self-destruction.

Having been in several positions of leadership, I have learned to openly admit gaps in knowledge and mistakes that I have made to my co-workers, supervisors, and colleagues. I also strive to create a safe environment for others to do the same. I see my work team as a collaborative group that shares its intellectual resources both to expand each person's working knowledge and to complement each other's work. Keeping an open flow of information, resources, and support helps everyone both individually and collectively.

I am sometimes tempted to share personal information about myself in professional settings in order to build stronger relationships. Exposing vulnerability in this way can sometimes backfire. It can be difficult to determine the most appropriate place to draw the line, and this varies from individual to individual. Trust your instincts and freely share stories and information about yourself to the extent that you feel comfortable and safe. Measure what you have to gain against what you have to loose and make an active choice about what to share with whom.

Our ability to expose our vulnerability is derived from our character, sincerity, sense of humor, confidence, and courage. When our core is strong, we remain unwavered when the gentle breezes of exposure roll by. In fact, these experiences nourish our souls and help us grow.

As leaders, we are expected to stand out – not because we're perfect, but because we are willing to take risks. Be willing to try new things even when there is a possibility of messing it up. Take a leap of faith in yourself, and have a little fun. If you are consistently genuine, your team will be sure to catch you before you fall.

Vulnerability is itself a type of risk. Some people might think of vulnerability as shrinking or hiding in weakness. I tend to think of it as a loosening and opening up. When we are vulnerable, all things are possible, yet we resist it because of fear. We might be afraid of appearing foolish, out of control, or incompetent. But aren't we all really all of those things to some extent anyway?

When I entered a Ph.D. program after being an executive director, the center of my little universe, for four years, I had a really hard time with vulnerability. I was so used to being 'the one' with the ideas, answers, and abilities. My professors lovingly pushed me and I eventually responded. When I think back to who I was before the program as compared to now, I can't believe how small I was then. My head was small and my heart was small and their size was frozen by my belief that I had made it. I now realize how unhappy and unfulfilled I was at that time, and perhaps that contributed to this overcompensation. I now realize how small I am, and that makes me bigger. I am bigger because by realizing my smallness, my insignificance, my fragility, I am more open to growth. I am no longer perceiving myself as having made it, I feel like I have barely just begun. Starting on this path was a huge emotional and intellectual risk that required vulnerability.

Your Response—Vulnerability

How are you vulnerable as a leader?

How do you feel about being vulnerable?

How small are you? How big are you?

How will you take a leap of faith in yourself?

Value

All we have is this very moment. In fact, we don't even have that; that moment is already gone. And that one. And that one. And that one. Everything is in constant motion and transitory. As we dance in response to the rhythm of life, it can be easy to take little things for granted.

Every day offers multiple opportunities for love, for growth, for beauty, and for enjoyment, and these are revealed to us through other people, objects, and circumstances. At every moment, we are exposed to intra-, inter-, and extra-personal energies that have the power to transform our thoughts, feelings, and actions both in the present moment and throughout our lives. When we are open to goodness, we will find it everywhere.

We have to actively seek value when we feel challenged, tired, overwhelmed, angry, or otherwise miserable. The gifts of the universe are not always readily apparent to us, particularly when we are enveloped in negativity. It sometimes takes years of developing understanding and reflecting upon our experiences until we are able to recognize the good among the bad.

On what was supposed to be my first day of high school, I was raped. This event, and especially the response of my family and police to the situation, emotionally wounded me and shattered my young life. I submerged into a dark depression and did not begin to make headway for about five years. What were supposed to be the best years of my life were actually the worst. I was not only angry about what happened to me, I was stuck in a hopeless response that further damaged my psyche and soul. I did more damage to myself than anyone else could have ever done to me.

I now know that I would not be alive today, and I would not be the vibrant, radiant, energetic, positive person that I have become, if it were not for this experience. At the time of this event, I was already spiraling down a dangerous path. Without this intervention, I would have most likely either killed myself or been killed. During those five desperate years of yearning, I explored all aspects of humanity imaginable which developed my insight and understanding about myself, others, and the universe. Although this was the most tragic and difficult experience of my life, it has also taught me important lessons that I needed to learn in order to survive.

I would never wish tragedy upon another human being, but recognize that in my life, this was my path toward personal growth and spiritual enlightenment. By choosing to seek and understand the positive aspects of our life situations, our ability to graciously feel and express gratitude will grow.

Live your life filled with gratitude, wonder, and delight. Express gratitude for all the good in your life through stewardship, affirmations, prayer, and sharing with others. Take time to show interest in others and genuinely express your love for them. Express gratitude to others for all that they have shared with you through personal notes, words of praise, and favors in turn. Be consistent and thorough in showing appreciation for, and reverence of, the people, things, and opportunities that make up your life.

Your Response—Value

How do you express your gratitude and appreciation?

How have you learned from traumatic or difficult experiences? How has this impacted your leadership?

How do you consistently seek value and goodness in your life?

How can we effectively lead others through difficult times?

Beauty

Ben was my one true love. He was 36 years old when I met him; I was only 11. I never imagined that I could love someone so unconditionally and completely. A lot of other people didn't like Ben and they didn't understand why I was so taken with him. He was older and had a scruffy appearance. But to me, Ben was my entire world and I loved everything about him.

Ben was a lesson horse at a local stable where I attended camp and hung out after school and on weekends during my middle school years. I met him on my first day at camp and, though I hated camp at first and wanted to quit, I fell in love with both Ben and summer camp by the end of that first week.

Ben's age was obvious; his ribs and other bones protruded from his skinny, but sturdy, frame and his movements were slow but steady. But to me, he was the most loving, gentle, kind being I had ever known. I was only able to see Ben's beauty: his silky, long mane and tail, his fuzzy brown fur, the stubbly whiskers on his chin, and his enormous size and strength all impressed me. Ben got more attention and tenderlovingcare than any other horse in Allentown at that time.

I cannot imagine what my life would be like if I had chosen to only see Ben's physical challenges. By seeing Ben for who he truly was, a beautiful and graceful older gentleman, I learned about the true meaning of life and was transformed.

I am so grateful to my friends at the stable where Ben lived. They trusted me, an 11-13 year old child, to take care of precious Ben. Perhaps they saw the beauty in me, and that helped me to see the beauty in Ben even more deeply.

We are all perfectly imperfect. Horses, people, trees, and rocks alike share this characteristic. Imperfections are reminders of our humanity and a call to find and appreciate true beauty.

It is easy to become frustrated with other people. They don't always understand us or do what we think they ought to do. Focusing on other people's flaws may bring temporary relief when we are feeling hurt or disappointed, but doing so further damages our relationships and make us feel even more miserable in the long run. All people are beautiful human beings who happen to have flaws. This can be hard to remember when someone is really pissing you off; if we try, we can remember and recognize the strengths and virtues that person has to offer. Strive to understand their point of view and help them to see yours as well.

When I am feeling frustrated and stuck, it can be really difficult to see the beauty, good, and value in everything. I sometimes feel overwhelmed and frustrated when things are not going the way I had hoped. This goes back to my tendency to control. When I am controlling, I am only looking down a narrow path. When I let go, I can see the whole field of possibility and all of its beauty.

On a daily basis, recognize the voluminous beauty that surrounds you. When you see a field of dandelion, appreciate the beautiful color and healing qualities of this herb; don't think of it as a noxious weed. Seize every possible opportunity to appreciate beauty, if only for a fleeting moment. Cumulative moments of joy make a big difference in our lives.

Leadership brings with it overwhelming responsibility. Take the time to discover, appreciate, and celebrate the beauty in the people, situations, places, and systems in your life. Take nothing for granted and seek positivity – the lesson, the light, the love, the good – in everyone and everything. Use your influence and resources to illuminate these beautiful ideas, things, and people so that others may be nourished by the beauty in them as well.

Your Response—Beauty

Describe the beauty that surrounds you.

How do you make the world more beautiful?

How do you recognize and appreciate the beauty in others?

How can or will you use your influence and resources to illuminate beauty?

51

Expectations

I love movies about teachers. One of my favorites is *The Marva Collins Story*. It was through this movie that I was introduced to a phenomenal teacher from Chicago who believed in her students' ability to excel in school and in life despite the distractions of difficult a home life or learning ability labels. In her book *Ordinary Children, Extraordinary Teachers*, Mrs. Collins stated, "students like to be pushed. They want to do well. They want to succeed. And once they have a taste of it, they will never again settle for mediocrity."

Like students, our co-workers hold the promise of the future. Part of our job as leaders is to help them realize this both internally and externally. When sharing ongoing feedback about employee performance, we can collaboratively set goals that reflect an expectation of excellence.

Our organization and community can also benefit from setting high expectations. When we envision and work toward an alternative future, its fulfillment is expedited by continually raising the bar as we achieve progressively more complex goals. We can create a synergy among personal, organizational, and community goals through open communication and mutual support.

High expectations are not equivalent to unsubstantiated wishes. While it is important to always keep your vision of the change you wish to create at the forefront, recognize that the process of everyday life, and the needs of others, may not coalesce with your personal desires. Set expectations based on what you can reasonably foresee accomplishing based on your experience and wisdom. Break goals down into manageable tasks and engage the support and resources that are needed. Hold yourself and others accountable every step of the way. Raise the bar whenever a goal is achieved.

Reality does not usually catch up to our expectations in the way or on the schedule that we choose. Whenever this happens, reevaluate your goal to determine if it is truly in your organization or community's best interest. Examine the strategies and tactics that were employed and make adjustments to improve your probability of success. Be patient and have faith that, in time, things will work out for the best. Remember that you cannot always control the outcome, but you can control your input as well as your reaction to the outcome.

They say that people live up to their expectations. When we expect mistakes, obstacles, and failure, we create an environment of despondency. When we actively create a supportive environment that celebrates hopes, possibilities, and dreams, we create the conditions for personal and organizational success.

Your Response—Expectations

What do you really, truly deserve?

What are your expectations for your life? For your leadership? For your co-workers and colleagues?

How have or do your expectations limit you and others? How do they help you realize your purpose?

How do or can you create an environment that supports hopes, possibilities, and dreams?

Commitment

Some people say that G-d is always watching. Regardless of your belief system, you are always a witness to your own thoughts, feelings, and behaviors. Your core values and character are revealed to you through these manifestations.

Our thoughts and actions can be negative and damaging, or they can be positive and transformational. Negatives and positives do not necessarily cancel each other out in equal proportion; they both tend to hang around in some way according to our expectations. Every thought and behavior has a cumulative impact. We are a composite of all of these positive and negative forces flowing within us.

Other people are probably watching you too. People look to their leaders for inspiration and often model their behavior in response to these observations. The best way to get the performance that you expect of others is to demonstrate it yourself. Be cognizant of the impact you have and consistently set a good example for others to follow.

Every moment is an opportunity for success (living our purpose) and excellence (integrity). With each interaction and decision, you demonstrate your values, goals, and priorities. Make a commitment to nurture a lifelong relationship with excellence from moment to moment, day to day, and year to year.

Your Response—Commitment

How do you nurture your lifelong commitment to excellence?

How do you actively witness your thoughts, feelings, and actions? How do you increase awareness and make time for reflection?

What do success and excellence mean to you?

How do you demonstrate success and excellence, or purpose and integrity, through your actions as a leader?

Failure

If there is anything I have done consistently well, it is fail. Despite the heartache of unrealized dreams, negative return on financial investment, and embarrassment among my peers, each failure has been an opportunity for me to try something new, expand my knowledge base, learn more about my strengths, weaknesses, and interests, and prepare for even greater failures – and successes – in the future.

I once had a business idea that I felt would have a magnanimously positive impact on society. Having just won second place in a business plan competition at a local nonprofit in Philadelphia, I confidently crafted a business plan to articulate the many details of this idea. My goal was to deliver the plan to a successful, and incidentally quite wealthy, individual whose heart I felt was closely aligned to the project.

I took the train to New York and arrived at his office unannounced. I was told that he was not available, so I left the plan in a sealed envelope with the receptionist. Then I waited. And waited. I was devastated when I did not receive a response. As a last resort, I used my last dime to purchase two tickets to a show that fit the theme of the project. I kept one for myself and sent the other to him using overnight delivery. I sat at the show alone, and completely heartbroken, that night.

There are so many things that I did wrong, but I tried – in my own way. But the very worst thing that I did was feel like my life was over when I resigned to the fact that this project, which I felt was a total reflection of my life purpose, was not going to work out. Almost ten years later, I now see that this was not the best path for me, I should not have gotten involved with that person as a matter of self-protection, and that my interests and talents are far more expansive than I realized at the time.

A few years later, I self-published a children's book and rented out a space in New York for a book signing. I thoroughly planned and organized everything according to advice provided by just about every article around on how to publish a book and hold a successful promotional event. Nobody came. That's right — nobody. But this time, I was not devastated. I spent the evening talking to someone who worked there and he is now a very good friend — truly a kindred spirit. I also feel more prepared for my next book signing after this trial run and I know that if no one shows up for that one either I still have the ability to thrive.

Taking risks can be scary and daunting when we think about the possibility of failure. Unfortunately, failure is always a possibility — even when things seem to be going well. Life offers no guarantees, despite thoroughly planning every detail and working extremely hard. So why is it that leaders insist upon taking risks?

Consider the alternative. If we didn't ever take risks, social and technological progress would be limited and life would be pretty boring. Thomas Edison said, "I have not failed. I have just found 10,000 ways that won't work." Every time we fail, we also succeed. We learn something new about ourselves, our work, or our world. Calculated risk-taking leads to innovation, greater understanding, and social and intellectual leverage for future projects.

When you experience an unexpected setback, or a devastating obliteration of everything you have worked for your entire life, remember that this is an opportunity for you to reevaluate your intentions, goals, relationships, and methods. We only fail when we don't learn from these experiences or when we stop trying. As Curtis Mayfield said, we have to, "keep on keeping on."

Your Response—Failure

How do you learn from your failures?

Are you afraid to fail? Why or why not?

How do you define failure? How does failure define you?

What motivates you to keep trying when things don't seem to be working out?

Temperance

We have all said and done things that we later regret — at least I know that I have. In a typical day, I am sure that I unintentionally offend, hurt, or insult at least five people. I am especially weak when it comes to other people not acting in the way I think they should; I sometimes tend to criticize and complain with abandon.

Like love and compassion, negativity multiplies when it is used. When we unload our pain and suffering in unhelpful ways, others ingest this hurt and it impacts their feelings, communications, and interactions. Through careful self-examination, we can minimize the negativity that we dump onto others.

Our words and behaviors are influenced by our thoughts and feelings. Thoughts and feelings tend to run deep and are influenced by a messy and unwieldy conglomeration of past experiences and future expectations. Untangling and sorting through this clutter to uncover the love and light inside of us requires patience, humility, and honesty.

The Buddha and Aristotle have two teachings that are helpful as we navigate this and many other life processes. The middle way is a Buddhist belief that moderation will lead to enlightenment. Similarly, Aristotle encouraged temperance as a means to practice virtue. Both remind us that we are continually balancing what seem to be opposing ideas, values, and behaviors. With one breath, we tell ourselves that want to be happy and for others to love us. With the next breath, we say something hurtful or inappropriate that leads to the exact opposite outcome.

Cultivating awareness of our values, feelings, and thoughts and infusing them with forgiveness and compassion (of self and others), as well as gratitude, increases our understanding and ability to auspiciously translate our internal turmoil into external tranquility. Every moment is an opportunity to learn, change, and grow.

When communicating with others, think carefully about your goal. Is it to prove you are right? To change the other person? To find a mutually agreeable solution? To create better working relationships? To express your love and gratitude? Unexamined potential consequences of our actions can lead to the unintentional deterioration of relationships.

There are times that we will need to have very difficult discussions with others. Perhaps they made a mistake that resulted in your company losing money. Or maybe they did something that caused discord within your organization or your community. At these times, a few guidelines will help to keep the conversation constructive:

- Recognize that we all make mistakes. Perhaps this experience is reminding you of something you once did and you are remembering the way you were reprimanded. Explore your feelings before reacting.

- Pause and reflect before speaking or acting when you have that luxury. Meditate and practice breathing to gain perspective before intellectualizing and rationalizing things in your head. Consider all of the potential consequences of what you say and do.

- Be honest, direct, and sincere. Do not escalate, project your feelings, or accuse.

- Don't bring up the past or set things up to fail in the future. Focus on the issue at hand and resolve it peacefully.

- Listen intently to the other person, but also to your own heart.

- Be proactive rather than reactive. Continually work on building positive, trusting, loving relationships.

- Find a vent buddy, a person removed from your work situation with whom you can share your frustrations and challenges without causing harm

- Create opportunities to process and release your negative energy. For me, this includes writing, walking, appreciating wine (in moderation, of course), and napping on the beach.

In addition to saying things that might hurt other people, I sometimes say negative things about myself or fail to recognize the beauty of my soul in some way. This includes rejecting compliments, downplaying my abilities, and haranguing myself in front of other people. While much of this behavior is driven by humility, just as much is influenced by self-loathing. Negativity sent into the universe will follow us as a cloud might chase after the sun on a windy day. When we express love for ourselves, we are better able to express love for other people. As leaders, we are role models for many other people. By being kind and caring to ourselves, we encourage our employees and others to also appreciate their gifts and to share them freely.

It is also essential to frequently remind others how much they are loved and appreciated. Let others know how highly you value their contributions and are honored to have the opportunity to work with them. Intentionally create positive interactions and communications and let this be your modus operandi when working with other people. Let other people know how much you value your team; brag a little! Of course, always be sincere when complementing others. If you look hard enough, you will find something positive within everyone.

Create a climate of respect, dignity, and reverence for all people — yourself and others. By being proactive and positive in our words and actions, we can create a healthy, flourishing environment.

Your Response—Temperance

How do you process and release your negativity?

How do you balance positive and negative thoughts, feelings, and actions?

How are you kind and caring toward yourself? Toward others?

How do you create a climate of respect, dignity, and reverence?

Listening

When DJ Kool Herc founded Hip Hop, he realized that people came alive during the breaks – the momentary gaps in the music he played as a DJ. When finding any rhythm, the quiet spaces where there is an absence of sound, light, or matter is often what defines the tenor of the movement from moment to moment. When we are still and quiet, beauty and peace have the opportunity to emerge. In our stillness, life's true meaning is revealed.

Listening to our hearts, other people, and nature leads us to deepen our understanding, acquire knowledge, and grow in our wisdom. Listening is the process of accepting and absorbing what is offered to us and allowing it to melt into our being so that we are transformed. When we listen, we resist the urge to control and commandeer conversations and activities; instead, we allow everything around us — divine energy, nature, our friends and family – the opportunity to infiltrate and influence every aspect of our lives.

We live in a loud, busy world where it is easy to get caught up in a frenetic pace chasing after multiple ideas and things. Sometimes, we forget what we are looking for or, if we remember, we forget why it was important to us in the beginning. Give yourself the gift of time to reflect on your motivations, desires, and purpose to add meaning to your daily routine and to ensure that your actions are aligned with your deepest values.

Silence creates the space needed for new ideas to blossom. When we constantly think, do, and react, the creative process is suffocated. Silence and stillness provide the energy needed to invigorate inspiration and innovation. Your composed countenance will have a calming effect on all of the people around you, too!

There are many ways that you can find quiet time within your daily schedule. Start and end the day with a few minutes of meditation or prayer. Connect with nature by gardening, hiking, or birdwatching. Allow yourself a break when you are working — a real break. Pause and take some time to reflect during or after meetings before making important decisions. Take time to smell the literal and figurative roses.

Be still. Be quiet. Be open. Set a new pace in your life — one where you can feel your soul emerge in the breaks.

Your Response—Listening

How do you listen to your heart?

How do you create meaning in your daily routine?

How do you create silent spaces in your leadership?

How do you create quiet, reflective time for yourself?

Fortitude

Sometimes it feels good to take the easy way out. Avoiding conflict, pretending things are fine when they really are not, and masking our true values or feelings to make others feel better may help us to avoid pain in the short term; but in the long run, these disingenuous practices stand in the way of true understanding and transformation.

We can only expect to falter when we build our lives around a fragile foundation. Standing upon a strong foundation based on love, courage, and hope provides the centering we need to live by the strength of our convictions. As leaders, we often need to make unconventional or unpopular decisions that are met with resistance. The process of change may stir up uncertainty, anxiety, and even hostility. Knowledge and understanding of your own inner values, and consistently acting in accordance with those beliefs, will help you lovingly and confidently articulate your intentions, calm the fears associated with change, and move others toward deeper connection with your vision.

Resistance is often justified. Leaders can make decisions that intentionally or unintentionally cause detriment to workers, systems or processes, the environment, and communities. Although we have been entrusted with the ability to make decisions because of our wondrous experience and knowledge, we cannot expect to be free from misjudgments and mistakes. Even when your decisions are based on your deepest inner beliefs, allow room for listening and learning. Inner strength provides the confidence to be vulnerable and open to change. Imagine yourself to be a tree that is able to blow in the breeze, yet stay firmly rooted in your experiences and values.

Chaos and challenge sometimes define the leadership process and relationship. During these times, it is helpful to continue to integrate our foundational beliefs into our practice. Winston Churchill taught us, "if you are going through hell, keep going." Don't let a little turbulence keep your plane on the ground. You can continue to soar and move toward your destination when your plane is sturdy and your vision is clear.

Difficult times present perfect opportunities to strengthen our character and expand our repertoire of leadership tools. As we mature, we may find that we are able to survive and even thrive during increasingly more challenging situations. Rather than avoid conflict and challenge, we ought to embrace and be grateful for the possibilities they have to offer us. Problems are exciting opportunities to reaffirm our values, learn something new, strengthen our commitments, and discover innovative solutions.

Your Response—Fortitude

How do you strengthen your foundational core?

How do you integrate your core when you feel challenged?

How do or can you expand your repertoire of leadership tools?

How have or can problems create opportunities in your leadership?

Patience

This one is a major toughie for me. I am scandalously impatient. I want to achieve my goals and I want to achieve them now! But by failing to practice patience, I am shortchanging myself, other people, and the potentially beautiful results of allowing things to unfold without my incessant prodding and interference.

Waiting is not a punishment; it is actually an opportunity to reflect, meditate, pray, and realize the many intricacies and delicacies of the natural process of life. Lingering fulfillment of goals builds a sense of anticipation that arouses joy and excitement. When those goals are finally achieved, a greater appreciation for the results will ensue. This may be difficult to realize during the time you are waiting, but in retrospect we nearly always know that what we have created was worth the wait.

Great things must be done with great care. When we hurry or rush the process, we risk being sloppy and counterproductive. Experiences that are carefully cultivated with tenderlovingcare hold greater meaning and value than those that are expedited to save time or money.

Sustainable change takes time. Think in terms of long-term results rather than short-term indulgences. Meaningful relationships, sufficient resources, and efficient and effective processes are highly complex phenomena that, when lovingly developed and nurtured, will lead you toward fulfillment of your vision.

While it is helpful to continually reflect upon your vision and its meaning, both to you and to the world, it is equally important that we remain centered in the present moment. When we place too much emphasis on the past or the future, we miss out on the present or, as some people refer to it, "the gift." Right now, you are alive and alight with the brilliance of your existence; each breath is an affirmation that this very moment is only time we truly have to enjoy.

In addition to neglecting patience in terms of time, we sometimes lose patience with ourselves and other people. When people fail to meet our expectations, it is easy to react with interrogation and condescension. Remember that time is available to you to reflect before responding. While time is a precious resource that few of us have to spare, using it in this way will improve your ability to respond with compassion in the future. It will also build trust and understanding, preventing the current situation from escalating. Consider it a wise investment.

Your Response—Patience

How does or would patience benefit your leadership?

How do or can you cultivate a greater appreciation for the value of patience?

How do you stay centered in the present moment? How does this impact your leadership?

How can you more wisely invest your time?

Defeat

I really hate losing. When I lose, I sometimes feel inferior, ashamed, and defeated. I will go to great lengths to prevent this monstrosity from materializing in my life. Yet somehow, I seem to lose more often than I win.

This is because I am asking the wrong question. Life is not about winning or losing, it is about learning and loving. When we position ourselves to either win or lose, we always lose out in the end.

It is inevitable that things will not always work out the way we had hoped. This often happens for a reason. We may have been pursuing something that was not in our best interest, or that of other people. What seems like a great loss may just open up space in your life for a new adventure. Usually, something even better beyond our initial visualization works out for us in the end.

But of course you don't want to hear this if you recently lost something of importance to you. When we lose an opportunity that was truly meaningful, it hurts. If you are feeling great sadness because your dreams did not come true, allow yourself time and emotional space to mourn for what was not to be. Reconnect with your sources of joy, such as faith, family, and friends, to reinvigorate your passion for life.

Pursuit of increasingly challenging experiences will likely result in increasingly challenging defeats. If you are not experiencing sufficient failure in your life, perhaps you have become complacent and are not pushing yourself hard enough toward growth and change. Every failure is an opportunity to learn something new, expand our self- and socially-defined boundaries, and prepare for the next step. It should be welcomed with open arms.

It can sometimes feel like a callous slap in the face when we see other people realizing our hopes and dreams. One of our roles as leaders is to support others' growth — whether or not they fall within the domain of our daily responsibilities. We ought to support not only our peers and subordinates, but also our supervisors and those who are affiliated with other organizations. Think not only of your department or organization, but of your community and society. What is in the best interest of all? When someone else achieves something wonderful, we all benefit in one way or another.

All we can do is the best we can do. There are many situational and relational factors beyond our control that will interfere with our ability to realize our perception of what we want. Congratulate yourself for trying, and be grateful for the opportunity to play.

Your Response—Defeat

How do you support other people's hopes and dreams?

How do or will you know when you have become complacent?

How do you feel about the dreams that you have let go? Are they still inside of you? Do they merit your attention?

How do you continually challenge yourself as a leader?

Transparency

I can sometimes be a phony. I have good intentions, of course. I want to project a positive professional image and build others' confidence in my ability to lead. I don't want to trouble others with the challenges I face on a daily basis. But by suppressing my vulnerability, I am reducing my ability to form genuine relationships with others and inhibiting their ability to just be themselves around me.

On the other hand, I can sometimes be in your face with the hard facts of life. I love pushing people through reality checks based on my interpretation of what is and what ought to be. This approach can alienate others, make them feel trapped in a hierarchical relationship, and reduce others' trust in my ability to protect them and our organization.

Both approaches are a little extreme. Somewhere in the middle is an approach where we can exude the genius of our genuine selves, open to freely giving and receiving dreams, opportunities, and love.

Rather than changing who we are to fit the mold of our organizations or to be closer to what we think others think we should be, we can safely express our needs, ideas, and concerns with those people with whom we have developed a sincere relationship. Our goal should be to develop such a relationship with as many people as possible, particularly in our leadership practice. Others will likewise feel more comfortable disclosing challenges and desires to you. Critical information should be shared both ways rather than hoarded or protected. The relationship is reciprocal, engaging, and trusting.

We should also create ample opportunities for staff and community members to interact with us — both in person and virtually. Be highly approachable by creating a system for intermittent communication and remain continually in touch with others on an ordinary basis through physical space, email, or social media.

It is helpful to be cognizant of how others perceive you to ensure you are truly representing the 'what you see is what you get,' responsive, and accessible leader you aspire to be. A periodic 360-degree formal evaluation can reveal areas for improvement. If there is dissonance between what you think and what others report, don't be preoccupied with the results; simply use this information to education and improve yourself to the best of your ability.

When we are seen as transparent, we improve our relationships and our ability to work and play together. Admit your mistakes, share your hopes and dreams, and unveil your insecurities with those who trust and value your leadership. Offer them the opportunity to do the same, and respond with love and care.

—

Your Response—Transparency

How do you share with others through your leadership?

Are you seen as transparent? When and by whom? Why or why not?

How do you create space for others to safely express their suggestions and concerns?

How do you create space to freely share dreams, opportunities, and love?

Optimism

From time to time, I lose sight of the perfection inside and all around me. We are constantly bombarded with negative words and images that can sap the strength out of even the most resilient people. Yet, we are surrounded by goodness, beauty, and love – if we only look for it and allow it to soak into our souls.

Negativity is like a cancer that exponentially grows and spreads. Unlike cancer, it is a disease that is extremely contagious; its afterlife is highly contaminated and dangerous.

Fire is a destructive force that extinguishes both natural and built objects – even people. Yet, it is also part of a natural cleansing process that can be beneficial, even essential. The Greek philosopher Heraclitus thought that fire defined the ongoing process of all life.

Destruction can lead to renewal; devastation can help us envision hope. Like other refuse, negativity can be composted. Mix it up with love, compassion, and forgiveness and the negativity you absorb will serve as fertilizer for many beautiful flowers in the world.

When things are bleak and you feel down, envision the alternative. Take small, manageable steps toward that vision and notice how good you feel as you move in that direction slowly but surely. Recognize your fears, uncertainties, and other constraints and allow good to flow through you and all you do. Stay focused on solutions. Recognize any mistakes that were made and correct them so it doesn't happen again.

Dream as big as the wide-open sky. See the potential for change in every problem. Radiate positive vibes as you go through the day. Open up to the possibilities of the universe — not just for you, but for all people. Encourage others to move through their negativity, a natural response to our seemingly tumultuous world, toward light and love.

Your Response—Optimism

How do you connect with the perfection inside and all around you?

Do you see the potential for change in every problem? Why or why not?

How do you open up to the possibilities of the universe?

How do you radiate positive vibes throughout the day?

Flow

When I sat down at my desk this morning, I confronted my lengthy list detailing what I expected to achieve today. I also have many running lists in my head of what I plan to achieve with certain projects and in certain timeframes.

With such rigid expectations for every moment of every day, I am potentially missing out on miracles. I may not notice the birds chirping, children peacefully playing, and beautiful sunset if I am absorbed in my relatively narrow vision for the day. I might also miss out on opportunities to expand my vision and goals, engage in transformative conversation with another person, or participate in a wondrous experience.

Being flexible prepares us to be open to new ideas and opportunities along our path. We sometimes feel attached to our goals or to the process we have chosen to achieve those goals. As we invite universal wisdom to inspire us, we may find it necessary to eliminate or change our goals. Things often do not end up the way we expect; many times, the situation revealed is even better than what we had imagined. Accept the outcomes and consequences with love and humility.

Go with the flow. Resist attempting to control outcomes and other people; this exercise in futility will lead us to feel frustrated and disappointed. Focus your energy on those things you can control – your thoughts, feelings, actions, and, to some extent, your environment.

Keeping an open heart and mind allows us to see unknowns for what they truly are — exciting possibilities. As life evolves, our purpose becomes more clear and we become more comfortable with ambiguity and uncertainty.

Goals are not bad; in fact, they are very helpful tools! When you set goals, ensure that they are aligned with both your deepest convictions and your wildest dreams. Monitor your progress toward your goals and reevaluate their legitimacy and usefulness on a regular basis. Allow yourself to be influenced by your experiences, other people, and inner wisdom that emerges. Plan your path, engage support, set your intention, and see what happens. If things don't work out as anticipated, feel confident in the knowledge that you have the power to change your goals and be comforted by the wisdom you have absorbed along the way.

Your Response—Flow

How do you allow miracles into your life?

Are your goals open or closed? How does this impact your leadership?

How do you feel about change? Do you welcome it or chase it away?

How do you feel about the unknowns in your life? Do you see them as possibilities or as threats to be controlled?

Flexibility

We get stuck in many ruts throughout our lives, both personally and professionally. One of them is sticking to people and places with which we are most familiar. This is often a result of logistics, convenience, and habit; however, it may also indicate underlying biases or fears.

Labels are superfluously used to describe things that are both familiar and strange. For example, we distinguish between good and bad neighborhoods, poor and rich people, and brilliant and ignorant ideas. Each of these descriptors carries with it the weight of preconceived ideas that may or not be accurate. Either way, labels often serve as a hidden social code that limit what you can and can't do or with whom you will or will not associate.

Because we are often bound to particular social circles or geographic areas, we have to be intentional about breaking down those boundaries. Travel to a neighborhood that you have considered off limits. Visit a library or public park to get a feel for the culture. How do you feel? What is the root of those feelings? Would you want others to feel that way on your turf? Do you feel that you are somehow superior or inferior to the people who live, work, and play there? And, most importantly, how can you use your influence as a leader to build relationships and change prejudicial attitudes and behaviors?

There are many other ways to exercise social flexibility. Here are a few ideas:

- Go to a religious service of a faith that is unfamiliar to you

- Visit a new restaurant and order a food you have never tried before

- Cultivate diverse friendships and bring people together across boundaries

- Travel to a faraway destination that opens your eyes to the multiplicity of human beliefs and folkways

- Take a friend with you so that you can learn together

Be intentional in creating new parameters to frame your understanding of the world. Take calculated risks to expand your social repertoire. Before you jump into a pool, you can anticipate the results by looking through the clear water to the bottom and testing the temperature with your toe. Yet, the exhilaration of the water engulfing your body is always somewhat of a pleasant surprise. You can expect similar results when you expand your social and environmental horizons.

What frightens you? Bungee jumping? Holding a snake? Calling that man of your dreams? Go for it! What have you got to lose but your fear and inhibitions?

Building a portfolio of diverse life experiences will make you a more flexible and adventurous leader. You'll also be much more amusing at cocktail parties.

Your Response—Flexibility

How do you use labels in your leadership? Are these limiting or freeing?

How do you intentionally break down boundaries through your leadership?

How do you exercise social flexibility?

How do you experience adventure and excitement through your leadership?

Fear

I once got a really nice email message from a program officer at a major foundation. She asked if we could schedule a phone meeting to discuss the consulting services offered by The Fruition Coalition. I was happy about the opportunity and honored to have been considered in this way. Then the fear set in. In the week between scheduling the meeting and the scheduled meeting time, I felt overwhelmed with dread, fear, and anxiety whenever I thought about it. I was very aware of these complex feelings and mystified by the paradox. I should be ecstatic, excited, and hopeful. Why was I feeling so bad when I should be feeling so good?

I examined the possible underlying sources of my fear. Perhaps I was afraid of failure; the phone call might not go well and the foundation might choose not to work with me. I could have also been afraid of success; having a productive phone conversation may have led to more work which would have been difficult to fit into my already hectic schedule. Maybe it was the tone set by the program officer; did I really still have apprehension of, and contempt for, people in positions of authority even though I had long before become one of them? One final thought crossed my mind: I may have misinterpreted my physiological and psychic signals based on a greater familiarity and comfort level with failure than success. Filled with eager anticipation and exhilaration, my switch flipped to afraid and retreating as a conditioned response.

I am still not positive about the true source of my fear. But by facing my fear and taking the time to seek greater understanding, I gained insight into my human complexities and felt more capable of effectively managing and transforming fear in the future.

It is quite natural to feel fear in a variety of situations. The more frequently we experience and process fear, the better able we will be to transcend this negative reaction and solidify our confidence and ability to remain in control. Fears have the tendency to drive negative behaviors, but by facing them we can position ourselves to make more meaningful and insightful decisions.

Fear is nothing to be afraid of. Embrace and love your fears. Recognize that it is natural. Invite them in and get to know them. Show your fearful side lovingkindness and compassion. Seek understanding of the root causes of your fear and clean up the residue from those turbulent times.

By living in the present moment, we can minimize the manifestation of fearful thoughts and feelings. Fear and anxiety tend to originate from memories of past experiences and anticipation of what the future will bring. Right now, at this very moment, you are a whole and complete human being with everything you need to survive and thrive.

For those of you who have a habit of worrying (like me), staying present can be a challenge. Meditation, prayer, or quiet reflection time can be helpful. You can also try to direct that recurrent stream of ridiculous ideas into a more productive train of thought. Ask yourself, "What is the worst that can happen?" and, "What else can go wrong?". Consider each response individually. Ask, "If this happens, so what?" Think about the consequence of this fear becoming a reality. Keep asking yourself, "so what?" until the impact seems insignificant, or at least manageable.

Let's apply this exercise to my example of the phone meeting with a foundation program officer:

What is the worst that can happen?

The program officer won't like me. She'll think I'm not as accomplished as other consultants she works with. She won't recommend my work to grantees.

So what?

This contact will not result in new work opportunities.

So what?

I will have to keep searching for new organizations to work with.

So what?

This is what I should be doing anyway. I'll be OK.

Your Response—Fear

Are you afraid of success? How does this limit or impact your leadership?

Are you equally comfortable with success and failure? Why or why not?

How do fear and anxiety manifest in your leadership?

What do you worry about? How does this impact your leadership? Your life? Your health?

Self-Care

I once participated in a writing residency to focus my attention on Limitless Loving Leadership. The first few days were highly unproductive, because I arrived physically, emotionally, and intellectually exhausted. During the previous months, I worked full time in a demanding job, took two classes in a doctoral program (for which I received As), taught two undergraduate classes, did some consulting work, and tried to be a reasonably attentive friend and family member. Not long before my arrival, I experienced a 17-day menstrual cycle. As soon as it ended, I started to feel the physical and emotional symptoms of PMS. I realized that I had stressed myself to the point of literally throwing my body off of its natural rhythms.

While my expectations for the residency were to produce a great volume of exceptionally well-written and profoundly influential pages, I now know that the most helpful outcome of this residency will be the opportunity to reconnect with my inner harmony and rebalance my life. I have chosen to pay attention to the warning signals my body sent out when it knew it could not reason with me intellectually. My soul compassionately whispered to me, trying to tell me to take it easy (as were my friends and family), but selfish me refused to listen. If I did hear anything at all, I did not honor my basic needs by changing my behavior.

I had a lot of fun during that writing residency. I loved lazing on the lovely porches, petting the sweet puppy who lived there, and sampling the delectable treasures of the other resident who was an amazing cook. On our last day, when we could have immersed ourselves our work, we decided to take off and feed the muse. We traveled throughout the county, vising wineries and breweries (but of course not drinking too much that it was unsafe to drive). It was such a beautiful, relaxing time. I still look upon my week at the writing residency as a time of deep renewal that to this day calms and inspires me. Experiences such as those are really important for our mental, emotional, physical, and spiritual well-being.

As leaders, we are responsible for ourselves as well as for the impact that we have on other people. We want to cherish them, support them, and nurture them so that they can succeed. But if we do not do the same for ourselves, our reservoir of love and compassion will be depleted. We may even grow to resent offering tenderlovingcare to others. If helping others is no longer a joyous and enriching process, this may be a signal that you need to pay more attention to your own well-being. Taking care of our self at least as well as we take care of others makes us more effective leaders — and happier, healthier people.

Regularly check in with yourself to make sure you are living a balanced life. If you are not, do not wait to make changes that will improve your quality of life and therefore your ability to lead. Neglected health leads to the accumulation and condensation of negative energy that becomes progressively more difficult to expel.

There are a lot of ways that we can improve the balance in our lives. Regularly reward your hard work with enjoyable activities – or even the opportunity to do nothing. Don't let your work overshadow your other life commitments. Pay attention to negative feelings and respond by making changes in your life. Allow others to extend their care and love to you. Integrate fun, healthy, exciting activities into your daily routine.

Your Response—Self-Care

How is helping others through your leadership a joyous process?

What do you do to take care of yourself?

How will you know if you are imbalanced and in need of a rest?

How do you reward your hard work?

Intuition

Our souls gently whisper to us all the time. The gentle, delicate nature of those whispers can lead us to overlook or misunderstand their meaning. When we don't pay attention, the whispers become louder before turning into screams. They travel from a spiritual, to an intellectual, to a physical level. When we don't pay attention to our intuition, G-d may try to get our attention in more magnificent ways that integrate all aspects of our being.

One morning a few years ago I was getting ready for work when all of a sudden I had a vision/idea of leaders as beekeepers. I thought a little about the analogy and then put it out of my mind, to be explored later. That night, I went to a 'Heroines of the Bible' class at a local synagogue and the person we studied that night was Devorah. Her name literally means "the bee." She and her husband made candles to share the light of G-d with other people. Then she was appointed the first female judge of the Israelites. Her leadership brought peace back to the land and instilled feminine values.

A few months later, I participated in the aforementioned writing residency. One evening I went for a long walk and went just a bit further down the road than previous days. A little over a mile away from the house where I stayed, at my turnaround point in front of a church, I came across a beagle. It was skinny and collarless. When I approached him, he backed up as if he were scared. I turned around to walk back to the house and the beagle followed me. Eventually, he walked ahead of me. When I got back to the house, my housemate opened up the gate and the beagle ran out! He saw me and kept going, down the driveway, then down the road. The housemate said that the beagle was sitting with her for a few minutes. It's almost as if he was leading me somewhere, or wanted to make sure I got home safely.

I decided to take a walk the next day, walking a different route than normal. I was half way across a bridge over the Tye River when I realized that I had walked into a swarm of bees. I looked up and there were at least a hundred, maybe two hundred bees swirling about. I turned around to walk back the other way because I was afraid to walk through the bees. When I turned around, the beagle was standing at the end of the bridge.

I definitely took this as a sign that I should continue to work on this book, and that it, and I, will follow Devorah's legacy. When I have doubts about the purpose or potential impact of my book, which I often do, I think of this profound spiritual experience and feel comforted as well as motivated.

Now that you think I'm certifiably insane, a charge that I cannot completely deny, let me share something else that will blow your mind. Our gastrointestinal systems contain more neurons than our spinal cords. It is sometimes called our 'second brain.' Thus, our 'gut feelings' are biologically rooted.

When you feel something in your gut, it is likely a sign that something is very right or very wrong. Trust and seek to understand your intuition, then act accordingly. Our intuition makes accumulated wisdom accessible to us in a highly efficient way. Take advantage of this wondrous opportunity.

Your Response—Intuition

What is your soul whispering to you?

How do you respond to those whispers?

What do you feel in your gut right at this very moment?

How do you use your intuition as a leader?

Openness

You never know what might happen. Many, many years ago, I met a guy that I considered to be an asshole. He was a dynamic speaker, a passionate advocate for many of the things I also deeply care about, and had a certain magnetism about him; but he was still an asshole in my opinion. His obnoxious vocal intonation, suffocating ego, and ability to argue without relent offended my sensibilities. Soon after, he edited an article that I wrote. While I enjoyed working with him in this capacity, my opinion remained intact.

Four years later, I received a friend request from him on a popular social networking site. Soon after the friend request came the getting together request. I was surprised that he even remembered my name or who I was, and now he wanted to see me? I wasn't entirely opposed to the idea, but busy girl that I am, I blew him off. He did not pursue the meeting and we sporadically kept in touch online.

A few months later, I found myself suddenly lusting after him — mostly but not exclusively intellectually. We went out for dinner and had a great time. Was what I really experienced through him a shaking of my soul (turns out it wasn't, but you never know)?

I am the one who was an asshole. I was only able to see this friend one-dimensionally and my misinformed opinion was mostly based upon his public persona. I passed up an opportunity to strengthen a friendship because of my own biases and shortsightedness. I regret harboring unsavory feelings toward this remarkable man and denying his initial request to spend time with me.

Unexpected opportunities, relationships, and blessings are all around us at every moment. How many have you passed by today?

Imagine yourself to be an amoeba with a selectively-permeable cell membrane. As you move along your path, changing shape in response to the flow of life, allow good people and experiences to enter your heart and soul. Be open to new ideas that may add dimension, beauty, and fortitude to what you already know and believe. Generously share your time, ideas, and resources with others and be open to them returning the favor. Let go of preconceptions about who you are and who you ought to be; let life, along with its mysteries and miracles, unfold.

When we keep an open mind and fluid heart, there is a possibility that bad stuff will find its way in there too. We don't always have the ability to distinguish between what is and is not in our best interest when we have insufficient information or rush to conclusions. We may be too trusting and allow others to abuse the boundaries of our relationships. Be proactive in detecting, countering, minimizing, and eliminating anything that seeks to maliciously infiltrate your precious life. When your heart and mind have been usurped by savage invaders, lovingly envision a realization of your initial intentions and keep working toward that goal despite the challenges.

You can prepare to bounce back from these betrayals by developing your capacity to practice resilience on an ongoing basis. Resilience is your mental, emotional, and physical ability to experience inner peace in the midst of chaos. This skill can be strengthened through meditation and reflection, by building supportive relationships, and with repeated exposure to increasingly complex life experiences.

The delights of love, romantic or otherwise, far outweigh the potential risk of being hurt, deceived, or abused. Be vigilant and make self-protective choices that filter and repel destructive relationships and experiences. Prepare to effectively deal with painful situations, but expect wonderful things to happen as a result of being open and flexible.

Your Response—Openness

What blessings have you overlooked in your life today?

How do you keep an open mind and a fluid heart in your leadership?

How do you practice resilient leadership?

How do you let the mysteries and miracles of life unfold?

Wisdom

When I was a teenager and young adult, I consistently had a flow of good ideas — but no resources to implement any of them. I spent my days dreaming, writing, drawing, and creating (at least in my mind) an alternative vision of the future — one that was more inclusive, loving, and interesting than that offered by mainstream America. My visions and ideas were based on my hopes and dreams as well as my skills and things that I found interesting. I would design beautiful clothing made with organic materials and in the process provide good jobs to hundreds of people, make movies to illuminate social issues, publish a magazine (The Bee Line) for counter-cultural chicks like me, be a world-renowned jazz singer, and, most importantly, be a loving mother to 12 children. Anything and everything seemed possible.

Fast-forward about 20 years. I handcrafted a few pieces of doll-sized clothing using found material. I executive produced one 10-minute documentary about hunger. I have self-published several books and have dabbled with various blogs and websites, none of which have resulted in a consistent audience. I sang karaoke at a resort in the Poconos, and won second place. And, alas, I am still single with no children — but have two nephews and have co-parented two lovely girls.

Although things didn't turn out quite as expected, I made progress toward realizing some of my childhood dreams. I have also achieved many, many things that I never even thought about when I was a kid. The ideas are still flowing, but not quite as quickly — I have become too bogged down in the details of life's intricacies. I have a greater understanding of what it actually takes in terms of time, money, and networks in order to successfully launch new projects. Despite knowing about the challenges of creating and sustaining change, I am not discouraged and continue to be innovative and take risks.

As a mid-career professional, I have had many work and life experiences, both good and bad, that add dimension to my ability to make decisions and lead. I have also developed a diverse network of other committed professionals and have a strong working knowledge of systems and resources in my industry. I have confidence in my knowledge of what works well and what doesn't, where to go to for assistance, and who to engage when developing or implementing various projects.

Someday, I will be an elder full of wisdom. I will have even more experience, knowledge, and connections. I will have more precise insight, more fluid intuition, and a stronger sense of self-confidence. I may even have more time to share all of this with others as we work together toward the greater good.

You are probably familiar with common age-related assumptions. Young people are careless, inexperienced, and not dedicated. Elders are out of date, complacent, and boring. While there may be an element of truth to these biased beliefs in some cases, there are also many positive attributes that can generally be associated with both young people and elders. Young people are optimistic, eager to learn, willing to take risks, aware of new technologies, full of energy, and unencumbered by life's disappointments. Elders have seen and done it all, can anticipate the impact of decisions, have longstanding relationships with people and organizations, and have developed patience and understanding.

We have many gifts to share at all stages of life. Intentionally developing intergenerational dialogue, collaboration, and relationships leads to a better balance of creative decision-making and sustainable outcomes. This process may be difficult; you will encounter linguistic, ideological, and conceptual differences. Focus on common goals, build greater understanding among all age groups, and illuminate what each has to offer to create a climate of respect and mutuality.

Your Response—Wisdom

How do you bring the generations together through your leadership?

What do you have to learn from those who are younger than you? Those who are older?

What did you dream about when you were a child?

How do you nurture those dreams and the dreams of others through your leadership?

Daily Planning Worksheet

Today I will express love for myself through these actions:

Today I will express love for others through these actions:

Keeping an open heart and mind allows us to see unknowns for what they truly are — exciting possibilities.

Weekly Planning Worksheet

Loving actions to take this week:

Our souls gently whisper to us all the time.

Monthly Planning Worksheet

Loving actions to take this month:

Unexpected opportunities, relationships, and blessings are all around us at every moment.

Annual Planning Worksheet

Loving actions to take this year:

When we are open to goodness, we will find it everywhere.

Daily Reflection Worksheet

Today's thoughts about...

Love

Compassion

Integrity

Openness

Humility

Authenticity and Purpose

Passion

Dreams

Other

Let light and love fill your heart.

Weekly Reflection Worksheet

This week's thoughts about...

Love

Compassion

Integrity

Openness

Humility

Authenticity and Purpose

Passion

Dreams

Other

Take a leap of faith in yourself.

Monthly Reflection Worksheet

This month's thoughts about…

Love

Compassion

Integrity

Openness

Humility

Authenticity and Purpose

Passion

Dreams

Other

While the limitations in our lives may seem endless, the love in our hearts need not be.

Annual Reflection Worksheet

This year's thoughts about...

Love

Compassion

Integrity

Openness

Humility

Authenticity and Purpose

Passion

Dreams

Other

Approach every moment, person, and circumstance with a new mind.

www.ingramcontent.com/pod-product-compliance
Lightning Source LLC
Chambersburg PA
CBHW060349190526
45169CB00002B/537